KidCaps' Presents
The Cotton Gin:
A History Just for Kids

KidCaps is An Imprint of BookCaps™
www.bookcaps.com

© 2012. All Rights Reserved.

Table of Contents

ABOUT KIDCAPS 3

INTRODUCTION..5

CHAPTER 1: WHAT LED UP TO THE INVENTION OF THE COTTON GIN? 10

CHAPTER 2: WHY WAS THE COTTON GIN INVENTED? 16

CHAPTER 3: WHAT HAPPENED DURING THE INVENTION OF THE COTTON GIN?................................19

CHAPTER 4: WHAT WAS IT LIKE TO BE A KID BACK THEN? 24

CHAPTER 5: HOW DID THE PERIOD OF THE INVENTION OF THE COTTON GIN END? 27

CHAPTER 6: WHAT HAPPENED AFTER THE INVENTION OF THE COTTON GIN?................................32

CONCLUSION 40

About KidCaps

KidCaps is an imprint of BookCaps™ that is just for kids! Each month BookCaps will be releasing several books in this exciting imprint. Visit are website or like us on Facebook to see more!

Introduction

The cotton plantation was called Mulberry Grove. In the past, it had been used to manufacture silk and rice. After the Revolutionary War, it was given as a present to General Nathanael Greene by President George Washington, as a way to thank him for fighting so hard when he was a soldier. It was a nice plantation, but nothing too spectacular. General Greene later passed away, and his wife now grew cotton on the land and owned a number of African-American slaves, who helped her plant, harvest, and process the cotton. Financially, things weren't going too well. She couldn't plant enough cotton to make the money that they needed. If something didn't change soon, she (and other plantation owners like them) might soon go bankrupt.

The plantation owners couldn't afford enough slaves to plant large amounts of cotton and process it before it was ruined by moisture. The slaves themselves had a difficult time working with the small seeds found in the cotton fibers, and the long hours of work made them very tired. Factories in the north that processed cotton always wanted more, and they even wanted to sell to overseas clients, but it seemed that there was never enough. India, Egypt, and Argentina were the world leaders in cotton production, which made the new economy of the independent United States weaker than it could be.

Little did the Americans know that all of these tough conditions would change in the year 1793. Something amazing was about to happen at that little plantation called Mulberry Grove in Georgia, something that would change the world forever. It was the invention of a little machine called the cotton gin. We begin our story with a man called Eli Whitney.

Eli Whitney stood on the porch of Nathanael and Catherine Littlefield Greene's house located a little way outside of Savannah, Georgia. An afternoon wind blew across the large field, mostly empty now of cotton. In the shade of the many trees scattered throughout the plantation, slaves were sitting down, separating out the seeds from the white fibers of the cotton plant. It was hard work. Each bunch of cotton had four or more sticky green seeds inside. Before the cotton could be processed and made into thread and material for clothing, all of the seeds had to be removed. In one full day (about ten hours of work) a skilled worker could separate about one pound of cotton from three pounds of seeds.

For almost two hundred years, since the colonists arrived at Jamestown, Virginia, Americans had grown their own cotton, mainly for their own use. However, because it required so much work to process, the cotton farmers were losing lots of money. The slaves had to work very hard with their hands, and they didn't have a lot to show for it. Some types of cotton were easier to work with, but those types only grew on the coast, not inland. The cotton that grew inland was much harder to work with.

During the previous months, Eli Whitney had looked at the slaves working hard and had listened to the farmer's worries about their futures. One day, he had an idea: what if there could be an easier way to separate the seeds from the cotton fibers? If they could cut down on the amount of time spent cleaning the cotton, then they could focus on planting and harvesting greater quantities, which would mean more money.

With that idea, Eli locked himself in a wooden shed on the property of the plantation for about ten days.

He worked hard, but wouldn't tell anyone what he was doing. At the end of the ten days, he came out holding a small machine in his arms. Elis Whitney had invented the cotton gin. Now, during the cotton harvest in the fall, he would get a chance to test his cotton gin.

This little machine would completely change the way that cotton was processed in the south. However, although he didn't know it, this little machine would have huge effects in the entire world. National economies would go up and down, lawsuits would be filed, battles would even be fought, all because of what Eli Whitney invented in the woodshed in 1793.

In this report, we will be looking closer at this amazing little machine, the cotton gin (short for "cotton engine"). Have you ever seen one working before? Do you know what it does? Basically, a cotton gin moves the freshly picked cotton through a series of rolling metal cylinders. Different hooks and scrapers pieces pull the cotton fiber one way and the seeds a different way. In this way, what comes out the other end of the gin is only soft fluffy cotton, ready to be processed into thread, material, or any other product. The seed are collected together in the other side, where they can be made into oil, or planted again for the next year's harvest.

Although Eli Whitney was only trying to be an inventor (and maybe to make a little money as a businessman) he never thought that his product would affect people's lives the way it did. As we will see, the technology that he discovered helped to shape the entire southern economy and even led to an increase in the number of slaves living and working in the south. In fact, some historians have said that, if it weren't for Eli Whitney's cotton gin, the south wouldn't have depended as much on slaves, which means that the Civil War may never have been fought!

In this report, we will see the story of a man trying to solve a problem. However, despite his good intentions, he ended up creating other problems along the way. We will see how even the best inventions and the brightest minds are no guarantee of success, and we will also see how money makes the world go around. As you read this material, keep an eye out for the following main points:

- **Why was the cotton gin so useful for farmers in the South?**
- **Why didn't Eli Whitney ever make any money from his amazing invention?**
- **What local and world changes did the cotton gin bring about?**

Are you ready to learn more? Then let's keep on reading about the cotton gin- the little machine that changed history!

Chapter 1: What led up to the invention of the cotton gin?

When English colonists arrived in Jamestown, Virginia, in 1607, their task was simple: get settled in the New World and find a way to make some money. They had been sent from England with all expenses paid by the investors of the London Company. These investors had hoped to make some serious money with the Jamestown settlement. They had heard rumors of gold in the New World, and had seen how much the Spanish had brought back from South America, so they thought that maybe Virginia would make them just as rich. As you may know, the colonists were originally pretty obsessed with finding such gold. This obsession made things tough for them when the first winter came, because they had not prepared any food, and had arrived too late in Virginia to plant any crops. In fact, they relied completely on the local Native Americans (including the daughter of Chief Powhatan: Pocahontas) for help during that first winter.

As the colonists realized that there was not a lot of money to be made by simply looking for gold, they decided to focus on taking advantage of the very fertile land of the New World. They started to think about growing cash crops. Do you know what a cash crop is? Well, a cash crop is a crop that is grown only to be sold. You see, most farmers grow different types of plants: some to feed themselves and their families; some to feed their animals; and some to sell at a local market or to international traders. However, when a farmer decides to grow a cash crop, he decides to dedicate most of his land to only growing crops that can make him money. What kind of cash crops grew well in the New World?

Although the Native Americans had been growing tobacco for their own use for generations, the English didn't like the taste of it. They preferred the sweeter varieties grown in the Caribbean. However, Spain was dominating all tobacco sales, and threatened to kill anyone who sold tobacco seeds to a non-Spaniard. Even so, John Rolfe, the English colonist who eventually married Pocahontas, somehow managed got a hold of some of those seeds. He arrived at Jamestown in 1610.

By 1611, John Rolfe had enjoyed some success growing the sweeter variety of tobacco in Virginia. He named it "Orinoco Tobacco" and began to export it to England starting in 1612. From that moment on, the New World became a profitable investment for everyone concerned, and New World farmers started to look at the land differently. They would have to grow crops for their own use and for their animals, of course; but as much as was possible, they would also try to grow cash crops in order to make a little bit more money.

For almost two hundred years, tobacco was the most popular cash crop in the South. Everyone in England wanted it, and they were willing to pay a high price for it. However, as often happens with business and investments, it was eventually discovered that there was an even better cash crop that grew well in the humid southern climate: cotton.

Cotton is a plant that grows to between two and five feet in height. Once per year (usually in the fall) the seed pods (called "bolls") on the ends of the branches dry out and split open to reveal the cotton and seeds inside. Plants are referred to by their "staple length". What does that mean? Well, it talks about the length of the cotton fibers inside each boll. Long staple cotton is easier to work with (the seeds separate faster) but it only grows well on the coasts and on small islands. In the inland south, farmers found that it was more productive to grow short staple cotton.

During the 1700s, a lot of interesting things began to happen in the world. For example, something called the Industrial Revolution began in England. Do you know what the Industrial Revolution was? It was a time when inventors began to create all sorts of new machines to make factory work more productive. In England, where textiles (fabric and clothing) were very popular, this meant that more and more factories were opening up to produce clothing and blankets. However, this meant that the factories that processed raw cotton into thread needed more cotton to sell to the textile factories. Where was England going to get all of this cotton?

For a long time, England had been getting all of its cotton from India (who had come under English control). India produced good quality cotton, but their real strength was in manufacturing textiles (fabric and clothing). England wanted to use their own textiles, so they forced the Indian people to sell their cotton only to England and to buy all of their fabric from English factories. It was a rough deal for India, but a good one for England.

However, with all of the new technology that came together with the Industrial Revolution (and the increased speed of cotton processing) the English needed more and better cotton. After the southern colonies discovered how good cotton grew there, England began to show an interest in buying their cotton. Even after the American Revolution, the cash crop was so important that the independent colonies were able to keep their cotton business open with the English. The demand went higher and higher and southern farmers couldn't seem to grow enough.

However, as we saw in the introduction, growing cotton as a cash crop had one severe limitation: it was very labor intensive when compared to other crops. For example, when a farmer grows apples, he has to plant the trees, take care of them during the year, and harvest the fruit each fall. That's all. The same is true for strawberries, grapes, blueberries, and most other crops. However, cotton has an extra step: after planting the seeds and taking care of the young plant during the year, a farmer must harvest the cotton and then clean the seeds out of the cotton balls. This extra step is the most difficult.

Do you understand the circumstances that made the cotton gin so important? Farmers in the South wanted to produce more and more cotton, and factories in England wanted it! However, it was too labor-intensive, which means that it was too difficult and took too much time for a worker to clean all of the cotton that the farmers wanted to grow. Like we saw earlier, it took about ten hours of hard work for a farmer (or for one of his workers) to separate just one pound of cotton from three pounds of seeds. For a large field, that means that a huge number of people would have to work a ton of hours just to clean a few hundred pounds of cotton.

Farmers were looking for a better way to process their cotton. Although there were different types of machines to help, none of them worked really well, and didn't really meet the farmers' needs. Someone with an inventor's imagination and talent needed to design and build a machine to solve the cotton industry's problems.

Eli Whitney was that man.

Chapter 2: Why was the cotton gin invented?

We have already spoken a little bit about what led up to the cotton gin being invented (the need for more cotton and faster processing time), but we haven't spoken too much about Eli Whitney himself. Why was he the perfect man to get the job done? How did he become interested in cotton production? Let's find out.

Eli Whitney was born in the village of Westborough, Massachusetts, on December 8, 1765. From a young age, he showed that he had an inventor's mind. When the American Revolution broke out in 1776, young Eli Whitney (only eleven years old) was too young to fight. As the war dragged on, he eventually was the only boy left at home (his older brothers all went off to fight in the war). He worked with his father, a blacksmith. Do you know what a blacksmith is? A blacksmith works with metal tools. He heats the pieces up in large furnaces and then shapes them to make horseshoes, hammers, nails, and even weapons. The workshop that Eli Whitney's father owned made nails. At the young age of 14, Eli designed a machine that was able to produce nails more quickly and of better quality. Can you imagine inventing a working machine at only 14 years old? Eli Whitney was a natural born inventor.

When he got a little older, Eli wanted to study at a university. However, none of the universities taught technical courses like the ones he was interested in, so he ended up studying engineering at Yale University. When he graduated at the age of 27, he was disappointed that he couldn't seem to find work anywhere. He heard of a teaching job in South Carolina, and decided to see what adventures he could have in the South. He didn't know it at the time, but that trip that he took south would be the one that would forever change both him and the entire southern economy. On this trip, he would be invited to build the cotton gin!

Eli Whitney got on a boat to take him to the South where he would work as a private tutor. As he was sailing, he got to meet some of his fellow passengers. One of them was Catherine Littlefield Greene, who was about ten years older than Eli was. She was travelling to her cotton plantation in Georgia (called Mulberry Grove) which she had inherited after her husband had died some years before. Eli ended up tutoring some of the children of Catherine Littlefield Greene's neighbor, and a friendship formed between her and Eli. She encouraged him to spend some time with her and her plantation manager (Phineas Miller) at Mulberry Grove.

When he arrived in the South in April of 1793, Eli had planned to be a teacher and that's all. However, when his other teaching job in South Carolina was later cancelled, he accepted the invitation to stay for a while at Mulberry Grove. He wanted to feel useful, so he would go around looking for things to fix, like doors, windows, or any broken tools. When he heard the farmers speaking one day about their troubles with cotton, his inventor's mind was intrigued. He liked the idea of being challenged to do something that no one else had ever done before. Would it be possible? Could he really design a machine to make separating cotton easier?

Let's find out.

Chapter 3: What happened during the invention of the cotton gin?

Once Eli Whitney had the idea in his mind to build a better machine for cleaning cotton, there was no stopping him. He went to a wooden shed on the property of Mulberry Grove and starting working on it. The biggest problem was how to separate the seeds from the cotton without smashing them- after all, the seeds were worth money too. They could be used to plant future crops or farmers could even process them extract cottonseed oil (cottonseed oil is used for cooking or as an ingredient in recipes like mayonnaise and salad dressing). Many of the machines and tools up to that point had been made from giant rollers that squished the cotton through a small opening and left the seeds behind. However, many of the seeds were broken along the way, and farmers didn't like that.

While building his machine, Eli Whitney had a great idea (although some say that it was Catherine Littlefield Greene who gave the idea to him): pull the cotton away from the seeds using small metal hooks or saw teeth! These hooks or saw teeth could be mounted onto a large wooden cylinder that would be turned around and around using a handle on the outside of the machine. The cotton would be put inside the machine and would be pushed by the hooks or saw blades towards a screen. As the wooden cylinder turned, the saw blades would cut up the cotton and pull it through the screen. This screen had spaces that were large enough for the soft cotton to pass through but that were too small for the hard seeds. The seeds would fall back down into a collection area, while all of the soft cotton would pass through to the other side. Once there, brushes mounted onto a second roller would clean the cotton off of the blades and drop them into a holding area on the other side.

After ten days in the workshop, Eli Whitney had solved a two hundred year-old problem! He had found a way to clean cotton faster and better than ever before. Although some farmers didn't like the fact that his machine cut up the cotton as it passed through, they were still very impressed. Do you remember how long it took one man to clean a pound of cotton by hand? He needed ten hours! However, with this machine designed and built by Eli Whitney, that man could produce 50 POUNDS OF COTTON in those same ten hours. Farmers all over the South began to have little dollar signs in their eyes as they thought of all the cotton that they could sell to England. Why, if it was so easy to clean cotton (taking about 50 times less effort) then they could grow two, three, or more times as many crops.

The Southland was set on fire with this invention, and everyone wanted to use it. But, how would Eli Whitney make his machine profitable? In other words, how could he get some money for his machine? After all, it was his idea and he had worked very hard to make it successful. It only made sense that he should be rewarded for all of his hard work, right?

The first step that Eli took was to apply for a patent for his new machine. Do you know what a patent is? A patent is a legal document given to the inventor of a machine or other piece of work. It gives that person (for a certain period of time) exclusive rights to the manufacturing and sale of the described equipment. Eli Whitney did not want other people stealing his idea (and all of his hard work) so he filed for a patent in late 1793 and received it in March of 1794.

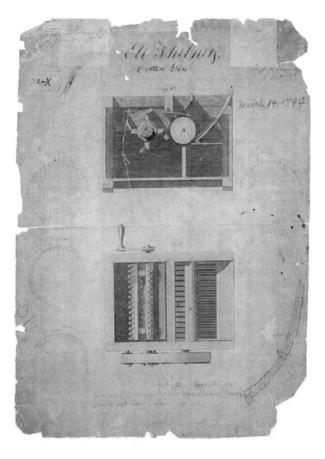

With this patent, Eli Whitney felt safe in knowing that he was the only one who could clean cotton so quickly and make it so profitable. Together with Phineas Miller (the plantation manager from Mulberry Grove) Eli decided to visit local farmers and to offer his services. It would take too long to build a large number of machines, so he thought that a good way to make money would be to go from farm to farm, clean their cotton, and then take a percentage of the cash crop as his payment. While it sounded like a good idea, Eli and Phineas wanted to charge a very high rate: two-fifths of whatever cotton they cleaned. If you know your fractions well, you can see that two-fifths is 40%, or almost half! While it's true that they would help the farmers to make more money, do you think that they asked for too much cotton? Well, a lot of the farmers thought so. In fact, because the machine was so simple, some bad people actually began to make illegal copies of it (we'll talk a little more about that later).

Eli Whitney had finally done it! He had looked at an impossible problem and had found a brilliant solution. Together with his friends Catherine Littlefield Greene and Phineas Miller, he had developed and built a machine that would allow farmers to grow and process larger quantities of a cash crop. You can imagine how good Eli Whitney felt when he put the finishing touches on his machine and showed it off to the cotton farmers. Life was good for Eli in 1793; however, within a few years, things would get very complicated for him.

Chapter 4: What was it like to be a kid back then?

When we talk about factories and farms, you might think that we are talking about things that only adults would be interested in, right? But did you know that a lot of kids had to work alongside adults back in Eli Whitney's time? Do you remember what Eli did when he was only 14 years old? He invented a machine that made nails for his father's workshop. In fact, for some time, he had been working hard with his father who was a blacksmith. It was not a strange thing for young boys and girls to work together with their parents.

The same was also true of African-American slaves. Even if they were quite young, they would be sent out to work in the hot fields. In the late summer and early fall, this often meant that they would be picking cotton. Have you ever seen a cotton plant?

Do you see the dark colored edges of the boll around the cotton? When these dry out, they become very sharp, like thorns. So imagine how tough it would be to spend a full day outside picking bag after bag of cotton. However, as you remember, the most difficult part wasn't the picking; it was when the slaves had to take out all of the seeds from the cotton before it could be sold. Can you imagine working as fast as you can for ten hours, day after day until all of the cotton is cleaned? The farmer might even be mean to his slaves, yelling at them or hitting them if he thought that they were working too slowly. Would you like to work in conditions like that?

If you were living and working on a plantation, whether as a slave or as a farmer, can you imagine how excited you would have been to see Eli Whitney arrive with his little machine? Although it didn't look like much from the outside, it would have been amazing to see how well it worked and how quickly it separated the seeds from the cotton! All of the slaves would surely prefer turning the handle on a machine to sitting down for days on end cleaning the cotton by hand.

After the machine became more popular, you may have started to notice some changes around you. It would seem that everyone was starting to grow cotton, and that everyone was looking to plant more. But, do you remember how cotton was planted and harvested in those days? That's right: it was all done by slave labor. So, if more farmers wanted to grow larger quantities of cotton, what would that mean for the number of slaves? Well, it would mean not only more slaves, but that slavery would not go away anytime soon.

Being a kid back then would have meant hard work, although it would have been exciting to see the new technology. However, knowing that cotton which was cleaned faster meant more cotton was planted which, in turn, meant more slaves were needed; do you think that you would have respected Eli Whitney more or less? Would you have looked at him as a smart inventor or as a man who made sure that slavery didn't go away?

Chapter 5: How did the period of the invention of the cotton gin end?

After Eli Whitney had invented his new machine, do you remember what one of the first things that he did was? He sent a request to Washington D.C. asking for a patent. Remember, the patent system in the United States was very young in those days- the country itself was only about twenty years old! Even though Eli Whitney had registered a legal patent for his machine, he still wasn't protected from all the kinds of bad people that wanted to take advantage of his hard work. In fact, the patent didn't really help him at all.

For example, after word got around of his new machine, some people actually broke into his workshop in order to take a closer look at his cotton gin. After studying its design, they figured out a way to copy it, and then went on to build their own (slightly modified) versions. Some of the thieves were so bold as to request patents for these versions- and the government granted them! Do you think that was fair? After all, weren't these men simply stealing an idea from another inventor and taking credit for it? In a few words, yes, they were stealing an idea. However, what they did wasn't technically illegal at the time. The laws regarding patents hadn't really been tested, so there was no way to know how much protection a patent really gave. Even though Eli Whitney fought and fought, he never ended up earning any money from his cotton gin. Finally, he left the South forever in 1804. Pay attention to his parting words:

> "An invention can be so valuable as to be worthless to the inventor."[1]

Did you understand what he said there? His invention, which had become so valuable to so many people, had brought him, the inventor, nothing but trouble. Although he went on to design and build other things and although he continued working in the manufacturing industry, Eli Whitney never again tried to patent his creations, feeling that it was a useless effort. To be honest, he was kind of right. Can you understand why he felt so frustrated?

Even though Eli Whitney never made any money from his cotton gin, he did gain something else: fame. He became one of the most famous American inventors, and for a time he was held in the same esteem as Thomas Edison and Benjamin Franklin. This fame eventually got him the attention of the American government, who hired him (with his blacksmith background) to make a huge supply of weapons. At that time, the Unites States was worried about an upcoming war with France). They made a contract with Eli, and he agreed to make a final amount of at least 10,000 rifles. During this project, Eli pioneered the use of "interchangeable parts",

[1] Quote source: http://web.mit.edu/invent/iow/whitney.html

which is a system where any part can fit any product. For us, in the age of automobiles and computers, this may seem really common; but in the days of Eli Whitney, you had to make each product one at a time. Because of this later work with interchangeable parts, Eli Whitney became one of the first manufacturers to work with mass production (like a factory).

However, there were other unseen and unexpected effects from his earlier invention, the cotton gin. As we mentioned, more farmers growing cotton meant more production. How much more? Have a look at the following graph:

There were 3,135 bales (weighing 500 pounds each)

American Production of Raw Cotton, 1790-1860 (bales)

Year	Production	Year	Production	Year	Production
1790	3,135	1815	208,986	1840	1,346,232
1795	16,719	1820	334,378	1845	1,804,223
1800	73,145	1825	532,915	1850	2,133,851
1805	146,290	1830	731,452	1855	3,217,417
1810	177,638	1835	1,060,711	1860	3,837,402

produced in 1790, just before Eli Whitney invented the cotton gin. Do you see how many were made five years later? Ten years later? Twenty years?[2]

Cotton production increased about 1000% from the time when Eli Whitney invented his machine to the outbreak of the Civil War. For some time, southerners had been relying on slaves to work in the fields. So when the cotton gin was invented and farmers everywhere decided to plant this cash crop, it was like a guarantee that slavery would continue as long as the government allowed it.

---

[2] Graph source: http://eh.net/encyclopedia/article/phillips.cottongin

In fact, look at the chart below to see how many slaves were living and working in the South:

Percent of Slave Population to Total Population, Southern States, 1790-1860

Year	Southern States	Border States	Lower South
1790	33.5	32.0	41.1
1800	32.7	30.8	40.3
1810	33.4	30.1	44.7
1820	34.0	29.6	45.6
1830	34.0	29.0	46.0
1840	34.0	26.7	46.0
1850	33.3	24.7	45.4
1860	32.3	22.3	44.8

This chart shows the percentage of slaves in the south. Do you see the increase on the Lower South after the invention of the cotton gin?[3]

As a result of cotton becoming more popular and more profitable, farmers in the South decided that they needed more slaves, and that they would not free the ones that they already owned. Eli Whitney had started working on his invention with the big eyes of an inventor, but he had finished feeling disappointed by the dishonesty of others. He never made any money for his invention, and had been taken advantage of by other people. More than that, as a Northerner, he did not support slavery. Can you imagine how he felt when he found out that his machine was helping to support this terrible practice?

Things had not ended for Eli Whitney as he would have liked. However, in the American spirit of never

---

[3] Graph source: http://eh.net/encyclopedia/article/phillips.cottongin

giving up, he continued on, worked with new projects, and eventually found his fortune.

Chapter 6: What happened after the invention of the cotton gin?

Internationally, things changed a lot once Eli Whitney's machine became popular. As more and more farmers got their own version of it (maybe even an illegal one) they began to increase the amount of cotton that they were planting and harvesting, which meant more slaves working in the fields and more money in the farmer's pockets. However, the changes weren't just felt in the United States. In fact, the whole international cotton trade was also severely affected. How so?

Up until this time, most of the cotton bought by countries like England and France had come from India. However, as we mentioned earlier, the quality of the cotton from the United States was better, and it was less complicated to bring it to England. With such a huge savings, England decided to buy all of its cotton from the South. Can you imagine how much that changed the Indian economy? Some people lost their jobs and others suddenly were stuck with too much cotton that no one could afford to buy.

However, in the South, things only got bigger and better. Because of the 1000% increase in the production of cotton, Southern farmers felt that they were invincible. In fact, although their economy was unbelievably strong, it still had its weaknesses. For example, do you remember what makes a cash crop different from other types of crops grown on a farm? A cash crop is not actually used by the farmer himself or the local community; a cash crop is grown for the sole purpose of being sold for a profit. Cotton is a cash crop. After all, you can't eat it or use it until it has been cleaned, processed, made into fabric, and sewn into clothing.

In the South, most of the land was taken up either by cotton fields or by tobacco fields. As a result, the Southerners had lots of money and had good economic relationships with foreign countries (like England and France). They also had lots and lots of slaves.

A few decades after Eli Whitney died, the Southern states decided to form a separate country, called the Confederate States of America. Why did they secede from the Union (and thus start the Civil War)? Well, a big part of it had to do with slavery and cotton. You see, the federal government, headed by Abraham Lincoln, was putting more and more pressure on Southern farmers to free their slaves and to find other ways of cultivating their crops. The Southerners felt that the Federal Government didn't have the right to make laws like that. They believed in what were called "state's rights", a term that meant state governments should make laws on things like slavery, and not the President.

Why did the Southerners feel so confident that they would win their independence during the Civil War? Well, they felt that the world wanted their cotton so badly that they would do anything, even support the new country, in order to get it. Look at this quote by a Southern politician (Senator James Henry Hammond of South Carolina) a few years before the Civil War broke out:

> "Without firing a gun, without drawing a sword, should they make war on us, we could bring the whole world to our feet... What would happen if no cotton was furnished for three years?... England would topple headlong and carry the whole civilized world with her save the South. No, you dare not to make war on cotton. No power on the earth dares to make war upon it. Cotton is King."[4]

Wow! Do you understand what the Senator was saying? He, as a slaveholder and a Southerner, felt that the cotton from the South was so important that the economy of England would have serious troubles if the supply was cut off. They felt that cotton was like king, and that they as Southerners were practically invincible. This attitude would be one of the primary causes of the Civil War.

Can you imagine? When Eli Whitney worked on his little machine so many years ago, he was just trying

---

[4] Quote source: http://teachingamericanhistory.org/library/index.asp?document=1722

to solve one problem. However, as a direct result of the technology that he helped to develop, slavery increased, cotton production increased, and the Southern states declared their independence. Historians have pointed to the cotton gin as one of the principle causes of the U.S. Civil War. Do you think that Eli Whitney had any idea what the effects of his machine would be when he was designing it? Of course not.

A little while after Senator James Henry Hammond of South Carolina said the above words, war between the Northern states and the Southern states did indeed break out. Were the Southerners right? Did their friendships with other countries guarantee them support in their hour of need? Did the world come crumbling down? Actually, what happened was a complete surprise to everyone, especially to the Southern states.

When the South rebelled, the North decided to hit them where it counts: in their wallets. One of the first things that they did was to put a bunch of ships in all of the ports of the South to block anything from coming in or going out. Why did they do this? This action would prevent the South from shipping out any of its cotton to England or France, and thus from their getting more money that they would use to buy weapons and to fight the North. The South was really hurt by this for two reasons: money and food.

With no income, it became very difficult for the South to get the supplies they needed to fight the war.

In fact, there were Confederate soldiers who went into battle barefoot because there was no money for shoes. Others had no ammunition, and had to wait until other Confederate soldiers died in order to take theirs. The Union soldiers were better equipped and eventually began to win battle after battle against the South.

However, that wasn't the only problem they were facing. Remember, cash crops are grown to make money, which is then used to buy food. Most of the farmland in the South was being used for cash crops, and only a small part of it was used for standard farming. When the Northern ships blocked off shipping ports, no food could come in. As a result, Southerners were starving to death in their own homes. When they finally began to plant food crops, they found that the soil had been overworked and that there were hardly any nutrients left. The food wouldn't grow. In fact, the Confederate soldiers couldn't even get enough food to feed the Union prisoners in camps, and many of these died as a result.

In Europe, the news of the war made everyone nervous. The South had expected England and France to get on their side, but both of those other countries had their own problems to deal with. In fact, they were more concerned with getting the food that came from the Northern states. What's more, President Lincoln had said that anyone who recognized the Confederate States of America (by doing business with them) would have to go to war with the United States. The South had made a big gamble that everyone would come to their side and fight with them, but no one did.

What's more, cotton was the most valuable thing in the Confederate states. In fact, the Southern states decided to base the value of their money on the price of cotton. At first, this looked like a good idea. When cotton was no longer being sold to anyone in Europe, there was a brief panic, and the price of cotton went up. However, instead of making a deal with Southern farmers, England decided to invest in Egyptian cotton. In fact, they put so much money into Egypt that they changed the national economy virtually overnight.

The Southerners were horrified to see the price of cotton go further and further down, taking with it their economy. "Cotton is King" was the slogan that had carried the Confederates all the way to war, and ironically enough, it was cotton that had made them lose the war. The cotton gin that had made them all so rich had made them trust too much in their cash crop. By the end of the war, over 750,000 soldiers (counting both Union and Confederate) had died, not counting all of the civilians who suffered also. It was a terrible time in American history.

Cotton, because of its high value, had completely changed the economy of the Southern United States and had even been a primary factor in its Civil War. However, as we saw earlier, other countries were involved. During the Civil War, England began to rely heavily on Egypt for cotton, and Egypt couldn't have been happier. They received large amounts of money and began to do lots of business trusting in their new source of income and their new customers. However, once the U.S. Civil War ended, England decided to go back to the South and buy the cotton from their old suppliers. What happened in Egypt?

Remember that the Egyptians had been counting on all of the money coming in from England. However, once the money stopped coming, the national economy got so bad that the whole country ended up declaring bankruptcy in 1876. Do you know what the term "bankruptcy" means? It means that the country doesn't have any more money to pay to anyone, not even to its own citizens!

That was bad, but do you remember what caused it? That's right: England went to Egypt because of problems with Southern cotton during the U.S. Civil War. And what caused those problems? Large quantities of production sustained by slaves. How did that come to happen? Because of Eli Whitney's little machine, the cotton gin.

Wow, do you see what happened? That little machine that was made in a workshop in Georgia affected millions of people living on the other side of the world. Eli Whitney could never have known how much his little machine would change the world.

Conclusion

Over two hundred years ago, Eli Whitney sat on the porch of Catherine Littlefield Greene and looked at her slaves working hard to separate the cotton seed from the fiber. He knew how worried all of the local cotton farmers were about the future of their industry, and he wanted to help. With his inventor's mind, he was able to design and build a unique machine: the cotton gin.

As we have seen, the effects of this machine weren't limited to the plantation of Mulberry Grove. Eli Whitney became an instant celebrity. Everyone wanted his machine and everyone wanted to grow cotton. Almost overnight, the struggling Southern economy became one of the largest in the world, and that eventually led to the U.S. Civil War. Hundreds of thousands of people died in that war and an economic crisis spread across Europe and down to Egypt as a result. All of this because of the invention of one little machine.

What about today? Well, cotton is still one of most popular and common cash crops worldwide. It is grown primarily in China and India, and the United States is still the largest exporter of cotton. Would you like to see how cotton is cleaned nowadays?

Do you see the machine in the picture above? It is a modern day cotton gin that is used to separate the seeds from the soft cotton. Do you know how it works? In reality, it is almost the same as the design made by Eli Whitney. There have been no major changes to the process, only the size and motor have changed. That is amazing! Can you imagine doing something that, two hundred years later, will still be used by people?

The world changed a lot after Eli Whitney invented the cotton gin. Before, cotton was often processed at home or in small factories. Fabric was woven by mothers and daughters, and clothing was made by each family. However, after the invention of the cotton gin (and the industrial revolution) large companies now could make huge quantities of fabric and clothing for lower costs. More people could have a wider variety of clothing. In fact, if you look at your clothes right now, most (if not all) are made from either 100% or 50% cotton. It is everywhere.

Nowadays, there are no slaves bending over and picking cotton in the hot sun. Much of the work is done by large machines, like the one below:

As with Eli Whitney's amazing machine, today one man can do the work of many. Technology is amazing, and it keeps making our lives easier. But, do you think that there are any lessons that we can learn from Eli Whitney and his invention of the cotton gin? Of course!

Eli Whitney, even though he was a very smart man, a hard worker, and a visionary inventor, never made any money from his most famous invention, the cotton gin. Why not? Well, as we saw, the patent system wasn't too strong back then, his design was quite simple, and he charged a high price for using his machine. With all of these factors, some very bad people decided that it would simply be easier to copy the machine illegally (or make very similar machines and obtain a legal patent) than to do business directly with Whitney. What's the lesson for us?

You have to be smart in a world that is full of bad people. No matter what you do, there will always be someone who wants to take away what you have worked hard for, and it is necessary to take steps to protect your investment and work. Eli could have asked less money, realizing that he could make more friends that way (and fewer enemies). He could have kept his machine hidden from the public until he was ready to manufacture many models of it. He could have sold the rights to another person and let them deal with the patent and headaches. Unfortunately, Eli Whitney did none of these things, and learned his lesson the hard way.

Another important lesson has to do with the consequences of our actions. You see, we never truly know how other people will react to the things that we do and say. For example, did Eli Whitney ever think that his invention would lead to the U.S. Civil War and to the collapse of the Egyptian economy? Of course not! There was no way that he could have known all of that information. However, history speaks for itself.

What about us? Every day, we have to make decisions and work on projects. We even have important jobs to do. We try to do our best, but sometimes we fail. In fact, sometimes we make things worse because we didn't think about the consequences of our words or actions. Eli Whitney has taught us to think very carefully about what might happen. However, we also have to learn that we can't control what other people do. Everyone has to make their own decisions.

The cotton gin was a little machine made by a simple man from Massachusetts. However, we have learned so much from it. We have learned about the power of money in the world, about protecting ourselves from bad people, and about unknown consequences of our actions. But most importantly, we have learned how much change just one person can bring about. Eli Whitney was such a man, and his little machine, the cotton gin, definitely changed the world!

Cover Image © Rob Byron - Fotolia.com.

Made in the USA
Las Vegas, NV
22 September 2023